Wisdom
from
the Witch
of
Endor

Wisdom
from
the Witch
of
Endor

Four Rules for Living

Tikva Frymer-Kensky

WILLIAM B. EERDMANS PUBLISHING COMPANY
GRAND RAPIDS, MICHIGAN

Wm. B. Eerdmans Publishing Co.
4035 Park East Court SE
Grand Rapids, Michigan 49546
www.eerdmans.com

Book design by Lydia Hall

Printed in the United States of America

30 29 28 27 26 25 24   1 2 3 4 5 6 7

ISBN 978-0-8028-8353-7

Library of Congress Cataloging-in-Publication Data

A catalog record for this book is available from the
Library of Congress.

CONTENTS

CONTENTS

FOREWORD

In reading Tikva Frymer-Kensky's meditations on the witch—the medium, the necromancer, the wise woman—of Endor, I was reminded powerfully of Tikva herself: a wise woman, gifted scholar, true mentsch, and trailblazer. Tikva showed women biblical scholars like me what was possible in a guild that was not overly eager to welcome us. Above all, she showed us through her words, and through her very own way of being in the world, how biblical stories, especially those about women, were not only fascinating in what they revealed about the biblical narrative in its ancient contexts but also had lessons for us today.

These same qualities are evident, in abundance, in this short book. Tikva's reflections on an intriguing biblical figure offer lessons that provide deeper insight into the story of King Saul's secretive encounter with this wise woman. We sense Saul's despair and the woman's growing understanding that despite the king's earlier proscriptions against necromancy, she had the power, knowledge, and wisdom to help him at this terrifying point in his own life.

On these pages, however, the wise witch of Endor, as channeled by Tikva, can guide us all, as perhaps she did for Tikva during her illness. The qualities that Tikva finds in the witch of Endor are those we all need in order to succeed in life and in our careers: determination, excellence, caution, and benevolence. We should all know our power, strive to excel, choose the moment, and win well; we would do well not to give up on our dreams too early but also to be wise enough to know that our goals may need to change. In doing so, we can hope to grow into magnanimity, with our spirits large and at peace with ourselves and others.

Most readers of Tikva's final gift will not have known her in her lifetime, but through this book and her many other writings, they will continue to learn from her about the Bible and about life itself.

ADELE REINHARTZ
University of Ottawa

PREFACE

Tikva Simone Frymer-Kensky—scholar, teacher, author—died at sixty-two, of complications from breast cancer, in her home in Wilmette, Illinois, on August 31, 2006. Tikva was among the first generation of women biblical scholars and theologians. Professor of Hebrew Bible at the University of Chicago Divinity School, Tikva possessed a broad scholarly and intellectual reach, ranging from ancient Near Eastern civilization to contemporary theology, women in religion, and feminist thought. At the heart was her love of Hebrew Bible. A gifted teacher and lecturer, Tikva taught thousands at synagogues throughout the country, at conferences and interfaith gatherings. In her lectures, she made the Bible come alive for her audiences, showing how the Bible both reflected and stood out in its Near Eastern setting and at the same time was relevant for the ages. Tikva was deeply committed to the Bible as a living document, as a source for teaching, inspiration, and guidance for us today.

Tikva was born in Chicago on October 21, 1943, the second daughter born to Berl and Elyse Frymer, Jewish refugees from France, who luckily were in the United States on a lecture tour when France fell to the Nazis in the spring of 1940. Ardent Zionists, Berl and Elyse moved to Israel with their children several years after Israel became a state. Life in Israel was difficult at the time, and Tikva's older sister Hanita could not adjust to life in the young country. The family returned to the United

States, except for Tikva's father, who remained in Israel until his retirement. In Israel, Tikva acquired her love for Hebrew. Upon her return to the United States, she pursued Hebrew and Bible studies at the Jewish Theological Seminary, and later she was trained in ancient Near Eastern studies at Yale University. Her experience as a woman seeking entry to the academy was a key factor in her transformation as a feminist scholar and theologian.

Wisdom from the Witch of Endor, found among Tikva's papers after her passing, is a new gift of Tikva's teachings. It is a shining example of Tikva's close reading of the biblical text and how such reading can draw out teaching for our time. In many ways it is a homily, a modern *midrash*, on the story of the witch of Endor. Tikva wrote *Wisdom from the Witch of Endor* while she was battling breast cancer. For readers of the

Bible, the witch of Endor is remembered primarily for her raising of Samuel from the dead and for her warning to Saul of the disaster that lay ahead. But Tikva took a deeper look at the witch of Endor and saw her as a marginalized woman who finally had her "moment," and in her character Tikva saw other marginalized people waiting for the moment that they too might be recognized. Tikva, author of *Reading the Women of the Bible*, saw the witch of Endor as a woman whose unique talents had to be kept hidden during the reign of Saul, just as so many girls and women through the ages had talents that were not fully appreciated or developed. To Tikva, reading the story of the witch of Endor brought back memories of her own youth (and adulthood) when she encountered more than one person questioning why she as a female sought to pursue her interest in the Bible and the ancient Near East and had to overcome many an obstacle on her way to becoming and being recognized as a scholar.

Readers will note that at various places in the text, Tikva uses examples of the different ways children are socialized to believe there is one way to be a "girl" and one to be a "boy." This language reflects her own experiences as well as the realities of the era in which she wrote. It has become increasingly common to see women in STEM fields, for example, and other progress has been made in affording people of all genders the opportunity to express themselves. However, still today we read about the difficulties women in technology face, especially in male-dominated fields like gaming. Today, Tikva would undoubtedly be less binary in her discussion of gender and would include examples of the struggles faced by nonbinary individuals and transgender people.

In *Wisdom from the Witch of Endor*, Tikva has left us a lasting life teaching from the witch of Endor—a message of resilience and graciousness, another example of how one's teachings live on and continue to inspire, long after one has gone. It was Tikva's hope that the story of the witch of Endor would inspire its readers on their life journeys, and so may it be!

Allan David Kensky
Evanston, Illinois
February 7, 2023

Meira Kensky
Iowa City, Iowa
February 7, 2023

Wisdom
from
the Witch
of
Endor

PART I

THE STORY

Samuel died, and all Israel mourned him. He was buried in Ramah, his city. Saul removed the necromancers* and the familiars from the land.

The Philistines were gathered and encamped in Shunem. Saul gathered all of Israel and they encamped in Gilboa.

Saul saw the camp of the Philistines and became frightened, and his heart trembled greatly.

* See Tikva Frymer-Kensky, *Reading the Women of the Bible* (New York: Schocken, 2002), 310–11.

Saul inquired of YHWH and YHWH did not answer him, not by dreams, not by the *Urim*, nor through the prophets.

Saul said to his servants, "Seek out for me a woman necromancer, and I will go to her and inquire of her." His servants answered him, "Now there is a woman necromancer in Endor."

Saul disguised himself and put on other garments. Accompanied by two men, he came to the woman at night and said, "Divine for me by the *'ob** and raise up for me the one whom I tell you."

The woman said to him, "Now, you know what Saul did—he wiped out the necromancers and familiars from the land—so why are you ensnaring me to cause me to die?"

* Frymer-Kensky, *Women of the Bible*, 311.

Saul swore to her by YHWH, saying, "By the life of YHWH, no offense shall be meted to you through this thing."

The woman asked, "Whom shall I raise up for you?" And he said, "Raise up Samuel for me."

The woman saw Samuel and she cried out in a great voice, and she said to Saul, "Why have you deceived me—you are Saul?"

The king said to her, "Do not fear. What have you seen?" And the woman said, "I have seen the divine rising from the earth."

The king said to her, "What is his appearance?" And she said, "An old man is rising, and he is wrapped in a coat." Saul knew that it was Samuel, and he bowed with his face to the ground and prostrated himself.

Samuel said to Saul, "Why have you angered me and raised me?" And Saul said, "I am greatly distressed. Philistines are warring against me and God has departed from me, not answering me anymore, neither through prophets nor dreams, so I have called you to make known to me what I should do."

Samuel said, "Why do you ask me, as YHWH has departed from you and become your adversary? YHWH has done that which he has spoken through me— YHWH has torn the kingdom from you and given it to your comrade David. Since you did not listen to YHWH's voice and did not exact his wrath at Amalek, therefore YHWH has done this to you this day. God will deliver Israel with you to the hands of the Philistines, and tomorrow you and your sons will be with me, and YHWH will also deliver Israel into the hands of the Philistines."

Saul immediately dropped full-length to the ground and was greatly frightened by Samuel's words. He had no strength as he had not eaten bread the entire day and night.

The woman approached Saul and saw that he was terrified. She said to him, "Now your servant listened to you. I put my life in my hand and listened to the words you spoke to me. Now you listen to the words of your servant. I will place before you a loaf of bread. Eat, so you will have strength, and then go on your way."

He refused and said, "I will not eat." His servants and the woman insisted, and he listened to them. He got up from the ground and sat on the bed.

The woman had a fattened calf at home, and she rushed to slaughter it. She took flour and kneaded it and baked unleavened bread. She brought it before Saul and his servants, and they ate. They got up and left that same night.

A BIBLICAL TALE OF

THRIVING IN HARD TIMES

isdom from a witch? A witch teaching a lesson in the Bible? The very thought sounds absurd. Everybody knows that the Bible prohibits witchcraft. Exodus and Deuteronomy even state, "Thou shalt not allow a witch to live." So how can it be that the Hebrew Bible presents the story of the witch of Endor and shows the witch to be one of the great and noble figures of the Bible? The biblical story of the witch of Endor demonstrates the strengths that enable her to survive and thrive despite hard times in a hostile society. In the story of the witch of Endor, we see a woman who refuses to give up her craft even though King Saul had made it illegal, whose skill makes it possible for her to come to King Saul's aid, whose wisdom enables her to apply her skill without risk, and whose be-

---

The biblical story of the witch of Endor demonstrates the strengths that enable her to survive and thrive despite hard times in a hostile society.

---

nevolence to her erstwhile enemy makes her a model of magnanimity in success. Determination, excellence, caution, and benevolence—together these attributes have made her immortal. These same attributes can help you succeed and thrive even though it seems that the whole world wants you to fail.

First, a very small language lesson. Deuteronomy and Exodus do not demand the death of all witches, despite the use that witch burners through the ages have made of it. The Bible demands the death of the *makashefah* (sorceress), the woman who recites evil incantations. Such a practitioner of black magic had the power (people believed) to cause terrible harm to others, to bring death or disease to whoever might provoke her. Fear of this ability made society call for her death. A woman who was indicted for sorcery and then condemned by at least two witnesses who actually saw her pronounce the harmful curse was to be executed. We are never told what kind of proof could show that the curse harmed someone. But in any case, the law called for the death of the sorceress, not of other kinds of women with occult powers.

The witch of Endor is not a sorceress. She is "the mistress of an *'ob*," master of an instrument for communicating with the dead. People might want to ask a ghost what is going to happen. Many people be-

> *The witch of Endor is not a sorceress. She is "the mistress of an 'ob," master of an instrument for communicating with the dead.*

lieved (and some still believe) that the dead live in the invisible world. There the dead can overhear conversations that let them know what has been decreed for humankind. From Ouija boards to tombstones to séances, people have tried to conjure the dead in many ways. In Homer's *Odyssey*, Circe, herself a great enchantress, cannot tell Odysseus what is going to happen to

him. She sends Odysseus to the very gate of
Hades to consult the great blind sage Tire-
sias. He is to dig a pit and pour libations.
Then he should let the blood of animals
stream into the pit (*Odyssey* 10.504–540).
Ghosts have no blood themselves and are
eager to drink blood. They will gather to
drink, and as the blood makes them tem-
porarily more substantial, they will answer
Odysseus's questions.

From Mesopotamia, we know of another method, equally bloody. (Remember Hamlet standing in a cemetery hold-
ing a skull, saying, "Alas, poor Yorick!
I knew him"?) A macabre cup was made by
plastering over the eye sockets, nasal hole,
and mouth of a skull. This skull cup was
filled with blood and was used to bring up
the ghost.

We don't know how the witch of Endor used the *'ob*. The craft has long since

been forgotten. Most people nowadays don't believe that it ever worked, don't believe that ghosts can be conjured or spirits summoned. But even those of us who believe in ghosts cannot use an 'ob. The skill of using it and even the knowledge of what it looked like have long been lost.

It is not the witch of Endor's craft, or even her skill at using the 'ob, that makes her such an important role model for us. Her behavior, her conduct throughout her story, teaches us her true wisdom—wisdom that enables her to rise to immortality; wisdom that can teach us, too, to thrive in hard times. We turn to the book of Samuel to look at her story (1 Sam. 28).

THE BIBLICAL STORY OF
THE WISE WITCH OF ENDOR

It is the last days of King Saul. As the Philistines muster to attack, Saul, a pious man, tries to find out what God wants. He goes to the prophets so that they can deliver a message from God. And he goes to the *'Urim ve Tummim*, Israel's approved dice-like instrument with which the priests could ask God questions. But God does not answer through any of the normal channels. Saul, desperate for an answer, knows that there is another form of oracle, one that he himself has outlawed. This is necromancy, a calling of ghosts by the use of a technology called the *'ob*. He hears of a master of this *'ob*, a woman in the town of Endor.

An Israelite king shouldn't be seen visiting an illegal witch, so Saul disguises himself and goes to see the witch of Endor at night, with only two attendants. He asks her to divine for him, but she reminds him that she can be killed for this illegal act. Saul takes an oath that she will be safe, and she begins to conjure. Immediately, she realizes that Saul is the king. But she continues and describes an old cloak-wrapped man coming up from the realm of the dead. Recognizing that this is the dead prophet Samuel, Saul prostrates himself on the ground. He reveals how desperate God's silence is making him. The dead do not like to be disturbed, and Saul has angered Samuel in death as he did in life. The dead Samuel denounces him with the same denunciations he pronounced when he separated from Saul during his life, and then he announces that the Philistines will defeat Israel and that Saul and his sons will die the next day.

Saul is devastated. He has reached the end of his strength. He lies on the ground, weak with fasting and with despair. Seeing Saul's distress, the master of the *'ob* approaches. Does she ask for a fee? Does she tell his servants to take him home? No, she tries to encourage him, and the story paints an amazingly flattering portrait of a woman who was, after all, involved in an activity that Israel considered forbidden. She reminds him that his task as king is not finished, that he needs strength to meet his destiny. Finally, Saul agrees to eat. Immediately, this witch becomes another Abraham. Like him, she humbly offers bread and hurries to make a feast, even killing her stall-fed calf to give Saul the strength he needs to go on to fight and to die.

The Bible knows that people who act in unorthodox ways are not necessarily evil. This outlawed witch is a generous and benevolent woman. And she is wise in all the ways that enable her to thrive in adversity and even become a biblical paragon of good behavior. This wise witch of Endor knows her own power, the use of an *'ob*.

> *The principles of her wisdom are simple to see: Know your power. Strive to excel. Choose the moment. Win well.*

She maintains and perfects her ability to use the *'ob* even though it was outlawed. She agrees to use her power only when she is sure it is safe. And then at her moment of triumph she is benevolent and gracious toward the one who had outlawed her. The principles of her wisdom are simple to see: Know your power. Strive to excel. Choose the moment. Win well. These four simple lessons are easy to grasp and hard to do. But once you master them, you too will be able to conquer adversity and to succeed in a world that puts obstacles in your path.

PART 2

The Lessons

Know
Your
Power

The witch of Endor has a unique skill: she knows how to use an *'ob*, a magical device to commune with the dead. Most of us have a talent, skill, gift, or power that sets us off from the crowd. Perhaps you can sew, do math, bake, run very fast, understand particle physics, have perfect pitch, know the batting averages for every major league ballplayer, can read Egyptian hieroglyphics, dance the tango like an Argentinian tango dancer, speak many languages, make a killer chili, sing like a lark—you get the picture.

When people are encouraging about our particular gifts, we thrive in their approval and are eager to polish our talents. But sometimes people are not so approving; instead, our gifts inspire fear, envy, or anger, and we begin to understand that the better we get, the more others may turn away from us. The moment we realize this truth is one

Most of us have a talent, skill, gift, or power that sets us off from the crowd.

of life's existential moments, those times when we must choose what to do, and, in so choosing, determine our destiny. We come to a fork in the road, and we must decide which of three paths to take.

One path is to deny the problem, to hold to the belief that if we get good enough, people will come around. And sometimes they do. The little African American tennis player who had no access to the "restricted" clubs in which tennis was played grows up to be Arthur Ashe, courted by the very clubs that used to be "for whites only." Young Billy Elliot becomes a principal ballet dancer who is watched enthusiastically by the family that had tried to stop him from dancing. The girl who wanted power grows up to be a mayor, a senator, or a governor. The "tomboy" becomes a world-class sprinter; the despised high school nerd becomes a great scientist. Almost all of us know someone or have heard of someone who achieved such success. Our mythology is full of such stories. And so, at this moment of choice, we may decide to persist defiantly, displaying (some might say "flaunting") our skills to those who clearly disapprove.

The French have a phrase *épater le bourgeois*, literally, "to shock the middle class," which indicates how scandalized people become when their approval is disregarded and what pleasure some take in scandalizing those people. This path may be very difficult when the scandalized react with an outrage that may be punitive. The very smart little girl who openly displays her love of learning will be teased in the playground, bumped into "accidentally," and even pounded on the head with briefcases. (Ah! yes; I remember it well.) The boy who raises his hand too often will be ostracized and even assaulted by the other boys. The divergent thinker may not receive rewards from teachers, or the too-independent filmmaker may be blacklisted or not find a distributor for their films. One may imagine oneself as an overcomer of obstacles, but in the meantime, one must develop a thick skin and become immune to the terrible trio: rejection, ostracism, and attack.

Knowing all this, our person at the fork may choose another path: to deny her or his talent, to abandon the ability that brought such dislike and learn how to be just like everybody else. The athletic girl holds back just a bit, enough to let her boyfriend beat her at tennis or in a race. Or she may direct her skills to a more socially acceptable route, abandoning ice hockey for field hockey. This happens less now, with more recognition of female athletics, but not so many years ago, girls were convinced to abandon the playing field, to leave basketball, for example, in favor of more "feminine" pursuits. In the world I grew up in, one never saw a girl endlessly shooting hoops as some boys do. Girls simply didn't do that, and there were no rewards for them, only frustration and dead ends.

Many of the gender rules have become more flexible, as children of all genders are encouraged to pursue physical activities. Computer science and coding, however, are another story. Even though society now may embrace women scientists, and special programs are established to interest girls in math and science, in the real world of most high schools, a girl who wants to spend her time writing complex code and interning at a gaming company can have a hard time overcoming the conceptions of appropriate female behavior held by other teens, by the science teachers, and even by the administration. Knowing all this, a girl at the moment of a decision may deny her abilities, "channeling" them into nursing or the more gender-open field of biology; a boy may play bass cello rather than the harp, or he may walk away from music entirely and go to business school.

There is a third path, the one taken by those who choose to continue to pursue their socially disapproved skills in private,

---

Whether you are by temperament openly defiant or quietly industrious, know your power and realize what an important part of you it is.

---

leading (as it were) to a sort of double life. They walk around in what I call Superman mode: the world sees mild-mannered Clark Kent, but inside, the Superman-like secret identity is full of talent just waiting to come out. No one knows that the quiet kid in class plays hours of chess every day, dreaming of becoming a grand master. He would prefer to be thought of as "nothing" rather than be ridiculed for playing chess. No one knows that the superpopular cheerleader studies vocabulary every night. If they knew what a "brain" she really is, they might label her a geek rather than cool. The polite salesman in the stationery store is secretly writing the great American novel, but he certainly doesn't let everybody know—why would he want people looking over his shoulder? People may not always reveal their dreams or their efforts even when they are open about other aspects of their lives. Whether you are by temperament openly defiant or quietly industrious, know your power and realize what an important part of you it is.

Strive
to
Excel

When Saul comes to the witch of Endor, she is ready. She doesn't have to consult manuals; she doesn't have to fuss around trying to get everything to work. There is a story that New Yorkers like to tell, about a tourist who got lost in midtown Manhattan. Spotting a man with a violin case, he concluded that this was someone who might be able to direct him. "How do you get to Carnegie Hall?" he asked, and, without missing a beat, the musician replied, "Practice! Practice! Practice!" Suppose that you don't want to enter the performing arts. You simply want to pursue a profession that aligns with your talents. But your teachers tell you that girls shouldn't do that, or society deems a profession inappropriate for women, or a seminary refuses admittance to queer applicants, or perfectly qualified people simply cannot find jobs.

Not so long ago, girls who wanted to be doctors were told that men would never go to a woman doctor; girls who wanted to be researchers were told that the chemicals would harm them; would-be auto mechanics were told that the career was for men; girls who wanted to be politicians were told that no one would vote for them. Not so long ago, African Americans were told that there was no room for them in medical school and that the only place for them in the courtroom was as defendants. Not so long ago, physically disabled people faced inaccessible school buildings and public transit. Even today, in some states, homosexual and transgender Americans are warned that no one will hire them as teachers; women are more commonly offered jobs as assistant pastors and less frequently put in charge.

The world is not fair, and when you are trying to overcome a barrier in order to succeed, you cannot be content with becoming as good as others. If you ever do get a chance, you will have to be ten times as good as everybody else in order to be accepted. There is really no place for a mediocre pioneer, a so-so barrier breaker. If you are determined to do something others do not expect you to do, you must work to excel at it. Practice, practice, practice! When the moment comes, you want to shine. After all, if you love doing something, then you want to be able to do it well. Not to be "okay," but to really show how valuable you, and others like you, can be. When the moment comes, you want to be satisfied that you have done the best you could and that, in your own small way, you have changed the world for the better. But be prepared! You may never get that big break. The book you worked so hard

> *When the moment comes, you want to be satisfied that you have done the best you could and that, in your own small way, you have changed the world for the better.*

to write never finds a publisher or, having been published, sinks like lead into the waters of obscurity. The people who award the MacArthur genius grants never even hear of you. Your finances may never allow you to quit your day job, or your arm may give out before your pitches ever break eighty-five miles per hour. The medical schools you applied to don't admit you; the law schools must have had a quota, for they too don't let you in. There are many ways that life can throw obstacles in your path, and some of them may be insurmountable. What then?

Don't give up too early. The mistress of the *'ob* doesn't let the law make her abandon her skills. You might be able to find a

---

Don't give up too early.

---

new path when your original path is blocked. You didn't get into medical

44

school? I know successful doctors who went to Guadalajara or another foreign school to study, knowing that they would have to pass special exams before they could become interns in the United States. All the law schools are full? Some very suc-

Sometimes your goal has to change.

cessful lawyers get their degrees by attending classes at night while working during the day. Setbacks sometimes require us to make accommodations: You might need to make a living; you might need to take care of your health. But you should not have to stop working at whatever it is that you feel defines you. Something you love should not be easily abandoned.

Sometimes your goal has to change. You want to do medical research, but you didn't get into a graduate program. You might decide to work in a lab as a medical technician instead. Perhaps you intend to try again for acceptance into the program later, or you may find great satisfaction in being part of the research team instead of its leader. Or, you could be a very good business executive, but you can find yourself "outsourced" if your company downsizes or gets taken over. If this happens, you might end up starting your own business and in so doing rediscovering why you studied business in the first place. People who are laid off from the jobs they love may try to find something similar, but they might have to compromise. In any case, you can make your now-changed goal still be part of the talent and interest that drive you.

And suppose you have to abandon completely your dream of glory. You have spent untold hours and a staggering

> *The process of working toward a goal has already made you different from people who have no special overriding interest.*

amount of money developing your talent or skill. You have practiced and practiced and practiced. But you never get to Carnegie Hall. You may someday play in a local civic orchestra, or it could be that the only place you ever play violin will be in your own room. You will never get that gold medal in skating; you won't even make it to the Olympics, or the Olympic trials, or the worlds, or the nationals. Maybe you will be able to teach violin, or skating, or whatever else you dearly love. But maybe not. Even if you are never a "success" in the way that you hope, it will not mean that you failed. The process of working toward a goal has already made you different from people who have no special overriding interest. Perhaps your dream has cost a lot of money and time. But they were well spent. The money, time, and labor that you invested have not brought you glory, but they have given your life a focus. They have given you energy and taught you discipline; they have made you a resolute and resilient person. All in all, not a bad bargain.

The witch of Endor never abandons her *'ob*, and even if King Saul had never come to her door, she would still have her *'ob*, would still be the person who defies public opinion to pursue that which interests her. But King Saul does come.

Choose
the
Moment

The king has come to the witch. What a great day! But the witch knows that she is walking on thin ice, revealing herself as a master of the *'ob* when the king has outlawed her craft. She could play it totally safe, denying that she has an *'ob* or knows how to use it. But that would be to deny her very being, to put an end to her dream of demonstrating her worth and the beneficial nature of her craft. So, much as she wants to help, she waits until it is safe. She chooses the right moment. She reminds the disguised Saul that the king has gotten rid of *'obot* and familiars. Only after Saul takes an oath that she will be safe does the witch begin to ask what he needs so she can help him.

"Build a better mouse trap and the world will beat a path to your door." Conventional wisdom promises rewards to those who labor alone. And Hollywood reinforces the message: "If you build it, they will come." We who face opposition or disregard eagerly grab these shards of

---

She chooses the right moment.

---

hope. People dream of the day when they can share their talents and be revealed as another Marie Curie, Niels Bohr, Sarah Bernhardt, Albert Einstein, Amelia Earhart, Marian Anderson, Eleanor Roosevelt, Bill Gates, Jane Hull, or Steve Jobs.

We recite their names like mantras, eagerly awaiting the day the world discovers us. If we have been studying, we want to dazzle with our brilliance, and just as important, we want to share our knowledge. Like Billy Elliot, we want our parents to understand and approve. Like Jackie Robinson, Marian Anderson, and Martin Luther King Jr., we want to break down the barriers that oppress us.

Dreams of glory, of satisfaction, of approval. Sometimes we need these dreams to

> *Sometimes we need these dreams to sustain us during the years we keep working in the face of public disapproval.*

sustain us during the years we keep working in the face of public disapproval. "Someday," we say to ourselves, "they will see what I can do. Someday they will want what I have to offer. Someday they will come to me, will beat that path to my door."

We want to shine for ourselves. But not only for ourselves. We also want to make our case. Those of us who have been struggling to make our marks in fields the world deemed not for us (because we are Jews, African Americans, women, men, nonbinary people, immigrants, fat people, or seniors) want to show that these fields are indeed suitable for people just like us. If we are working to be proficient in areas that society thinks are not suitable for anyone, as the occult arts or mystical arts were in the times of the witch of Endor, we want people to acknowledge that these are legitimate spheres of study. And if we have been trying to make our names in fields considered dangerous, like political action or magic, we want to convince the world that our fields are indeed for everybody, that they are beneficial rather than dangerous, that they will help humankind rather than hurt.

How much we long for the day that the world comes to us. We are so eager to spread the word that we sometimes open up at the slightest invitation. In fact, we may "come out" before it is really safe to do so. How we imagine the applause of others, the proud smiles on the faces of our parents, the high fives from our friends. We build whole scenes in our minds. You see a poem published, or a book of poems, and the family stops making fun of its "dreamer." You get a letter of acceptance from Julliard or MIT—even a scholarship—and the family rallies to send you to college instead of expecting you to work in the family business. You get a callback at an audition or a part in an off-off-off-Broadway play, and maybe people stop telling you to be "sensible" or "practical." Or you get a patent on an invention or make a breakthrough discovery, and people no longer laugh at the "mad scientist." Our dreams don't stop there, of course—somewhere in the back of our consciousness even greater scenes play out: an Oscar! A Pulitzer! A MacArthur genius grant, the Nobel Prize, the CEO of a Fortune 500 company, or even president of the United States!

Of course, we don't really count on that big prize. We believe it, but we know how slim our chances are. In all our dreams, the common factor is that we make it on our own terms. We don't sell out. We keep our day jobs and we keep on trying. And we want to be recognized for our efforts. We are longing for acknowl-

edgment, and we may share our dreams or
show our hand before it is really safe to do

---

*In all our dreams, the
common factor is that we
make it on our own terms.*

---

so. And if we do, we will meet with ridi-
cule, anger, or derision. Such a reaction
isn't total, and we may rebound with even
greater determination, but it is wiser to
wait till the time is right, till there is a good
chance that we will be appreciated rather
than feared or condemned.

In the book of Esther, Queen Vashti
wants to be treated like a person; she
wants all women to have some self-
determination. So she refuses to appear
when the king summons her—a brave

act toward a laudable goal. But Vashti has made no preparations; she has no power of her own to back her revolt, no supporters to storm the palace. As a result, she is simply removed from the throne, and the cause of bringing more power to women waited several thousand years. No matter who you are, if the world isn't ready for you, you may have to bide your time. Be safe and keep working until it is truly your time to shine and succeed.

Win,
Well

Aha! The moment has come! All those years of preparation, all those years of hiding your talents, of keeping your light under a bushel. No more people looking at you unknowingly, thinking how ordinary you are. No more people finding out what you do and getting angry at you for it or, worse, outright laughing at you. How many years has it been that people have told you that you'll never amount to anything, that a woman (or a man) needs something to fall back on, or that a man (or a woman) has to be able to support a family? How many years did you pretend to be ordinary or did you fight for your right to develop your talents, to do what you want to do? Years of so many people ignoring you, people reviling you. How many times did you listen politely to people telling you what you ought to be, how you ought to behave, what you ought to think? Everybody always seems to think that they know what is best for you. They never seem to realize how much they are insulting you, how much they invalidate everything you are, everything important to you. It is hard not to be angry, hard not to wish for the day of reckoning, for the time when people will appreciate who you truly are. "Just you wait—you'll be sorry but your tears will come too late." So fantasizes Eliza Doolittle, chafing under Henry Higgins's stern attempt to de-Cockney her. Someday, she dreams, she will be a great success at court and the king will ask her what to do with Henry Higgins. The moment of triumph is at hand, and Eliza answers, "Off with his head!"

Oh sweet and bloody fantasy of revenge! And Eliza is a willing participant in her education! She herself has come to hire Henry Higgins to teach her how to talk like an English lady, not realizing that he would set out to transform not only her speech but also the very fabric of her acts and thoughts. And so she plots her revenge.

Like Eliza, Jenny, the barmaid in *The Threepenny Opera*, dreams of revenge. She sings of the day a great eight-sailed tall ship will come and conquer the town. They will rescue Jenny, and then (in her fantasy), they will ask her, "Whom should we kill?" She will answer, "All!" In the movies, formerly mousy women turn beautiful and then systematically destroy the men who spurned them; or men, once bullied as nerds, become fabulously wealthy and displace those who tormented them.

It is almost a cliché: the meek will inherit the earth; the formerly scorned will destroy or, more peacefully, turn their backs on those who reviled them; the formerly powerless will use their new power to "get even," "settle the score," or "give them a taste of their own medicine."

But wait—maybe your fantasies don't run to revenge, and certainly not murder. But you do yearn for that moment of triumph, when your gifts are acknowledged and you emerge victorious or you save the day with precisely those talents that the world didn't want you to have. Ah, sweet moment of success! The toad has become a prince, Cinderella a princess, and the world is beating a path to your door, singing your praises and regretting that they didn't appreciate you sooner.

Many of us share this magnificent fantasy. The dream of success keeps us going when times are hard. Even if we tell ourselves that we don't expect rewards, that we do what we do because we have to, or because we love it, or because it is what we

> *The dream of success keeps us going when times are hard.*

are—even so, somewhere, I'll wager, lurks a dream of family approval, of public respect, maybe even of fame and fortune. But except for angry revenge fantasies, we rarely think about how we will act at the moment for which we have yearned. Perhaps, we imagine, we will be the model of graciousness, mentally waving at cheering crowds like Queen Elizabeth. Perhaps we will explain the secrets of the universe to eager reporters. Or perhaps, we imagine, we will smile demurely, shy in our moment of victory, the very model of humility, modesty, and grace. Whether we see ourselves as vengeful or gracious, the moment after is exactly that: one single moment. Our focus is on ourselves. There is nothing wrong with this—we have earned our moment in the sun and we needn't feel embarrassed or upset if we want to bask in it. But we can never live in adulation; even if we want to, the world wouldn't let us. "Fifteen minutes," says Andy Warhol—fifteen minutes and then back to the real world.

It is here that the witch of Endor teaches us her last and maybe most important lesson. There she is—the woman whose skill King Saul had outlawed has now come to his aid with that very skill. Oh sweet moment of triumph! We would all understand if she had told him off, if she had berated him for the years during which she had to hide, hearing her power denigrated by those around her. At least, we think, she could have said what Jephthah said to his brothers: "Why come to me when you didn't like me before?" Or she could have chanted "na-ni-na-ni-noo-nah" or danced the Debbie Reynolds "I told you so, I told you so" dance. But she does none of that. Instead, at this, her moment, she becomes not an agent of revenge but a paragon of humane benevolence. Seeing Saul destroyed at her feet, her thoughts are of him, not of herself. Without pausing to savor her moment, she focuses her attention on his distress and moves to succor him. She shows no concern for herself, no thought of herself as she seeks to give her guest strength to meet his destiny. She transforms herself from someone defined

by her outlawed gift, necromancy, into the
very image of a caregiver. Saul came to her
in need of her unique gift, and she showed
that her special powers have a necessary
place in the world. Now he has need of
her other gifts, those which we all can
share, and she shows that her power with
the *'ob*, important as it is, does not define
her. She is also a concerned human being
who demonstrates the actions of benevolence, actions of human kindness. Instead
of scorn, she offers concern; instead of
revenge, succor.

The witch of Endor is a wise woman.
Revenge may offer satisfaction for a min-
ute, an "I told you so" may feel good on
the lips, but "payback time" is a fleeting
moment. There may be a certain sense
of satisfaction that accompanies the "revenge," perhaps even a smile as you later
remember the way it felt to put others in

their place, even to "get some of your own back." But ultimately, the pleasure fades and the memory turns sad. Getting your own back stops seeming like such a good idea after all. Embarrassment over your bad behavior can color the memory of the event. From being one of the high points of your life, it can come to seem like one of the lowest. The sweet knowledge that you were right to develop your abilities turns sour as you realize that when it counted, you acted no better than those who had mistreated you. Revenge is a dish best not tasted at all.

But how about that other adage, "Living well is the best revenge"? Surely there is nothing wrong with reaping rewards from newfound attention and approval. If our success has a material aspect, who would fault us for lavishing attention on ourselves, buying ourselves all the things we couldn't before, indulging in some of the world's costly pleasures? If we have sacrificed our time to hone our talent, if we have gone without luxuries because the world didn't appreciate us, what is wrong with rewarding ourselves once we are recognized? Certainly, indulging ourselves doesn't hurt anyone, does it?

Alas, it does hurt someone—it hurts you. And it not only hurts you once, it

> *If our dream of recognition is bound up with dreams of material luxury, then no recognition may be enough.*

may continue to hurt you, damaging your self-esteem and distorting your self-image. "Living well" in our culture takes money, lots of money, and if our dream of success includes the money to reward ourselves with the "good life" we see in magazines and television, then no success may ever be enough. For there are many ways to achieve success in what we want to do, many ways for others to recognize our achievements. If our dream of recognition is bound up with dreams of material luxury, then no recognition may be enough. The approval of family and friends will not satisfy us, for it often has no cash value. Recognition of our efforts by schools, universities, hospitals, and the press also often has little money attached. We may never feel appreciated unless we win a Pulitzer, a MacArthur, or a Nobel—and maybe even these won't be enough.

The desire for luxurious living changes the nature of your dream. After all, you have not single-mindedly pursued money.

You may even have felt very different from the people who pursue our society's normal ways of making money. Maybe secretly you felt better than them; you certainly felt different. In fact, in order to develop your own talents, you have made monetary sacrifices. But if you measure the success of your unorthodox path by the same standards that you rejected in order to follow that very path, then you will always feel restless, always unfulfilled.

> *Your actions will turn*
> *you into someone you*
> *may not even recognize.*

But suppose you actually win fame and fortune—then can you indulge yourself? This is a situation few will encounter, but even here "the good life" presents problems. For your quest of your own path wasn't really motivated by such a desire, and if, in the moment of great success, you act as if it had been, then you will begin to change. Your actions will turn you into someone you may not even recognize.

And this is where the wisdom of the witch can save you. For she "lives well" in

> *We grow with each act until*
> *we are truly magnanimous,*
> *large of spirit, at peace with*
> *ourselves and with others.*

a different way, focusing on Saul's need rather than savoring her success. Benevolence—acting well toward someone else—also feels good in the moment, but, unlike revenge or self-indulgence, benevolence has an ongoing benefit for our well-being. It increases our self-esteem, causing us to see ourselves as capable of serving others. And it enlarges our spirit, for each act of loving-kindness builds our spirit. We grow with each act until we are truly magnanimous, large of spirit, at peace with ourselves and with others. Through her selfless concern, the mistress of the *'ob* becomes immortal. Her name has long since passed out of memory. What difference would it make if she was named Sarah or Hannah? She is remembered for her craft. "The mistress of the *'ob*," that very craft that she worked to maintain, and her story remind us that even people whose actions are suspect in their own day can be wonderful, magnanimous, and benevolent spirits. And so can we.

A FINAL WORD

There are no magic formulas to ensure success. But the story of the witch of Endor shows us what kind of success to long for, how to recognize it, and how to act when we achieve it. Her story teaches us four lessons. These are worth repeating time and again:

1. Know your power.
2. Strive to excel.
3. Choose the moment.
4. Win well.

When applied together, these four lessons offer a full, rich life and a path for thriving even when times are very hard.